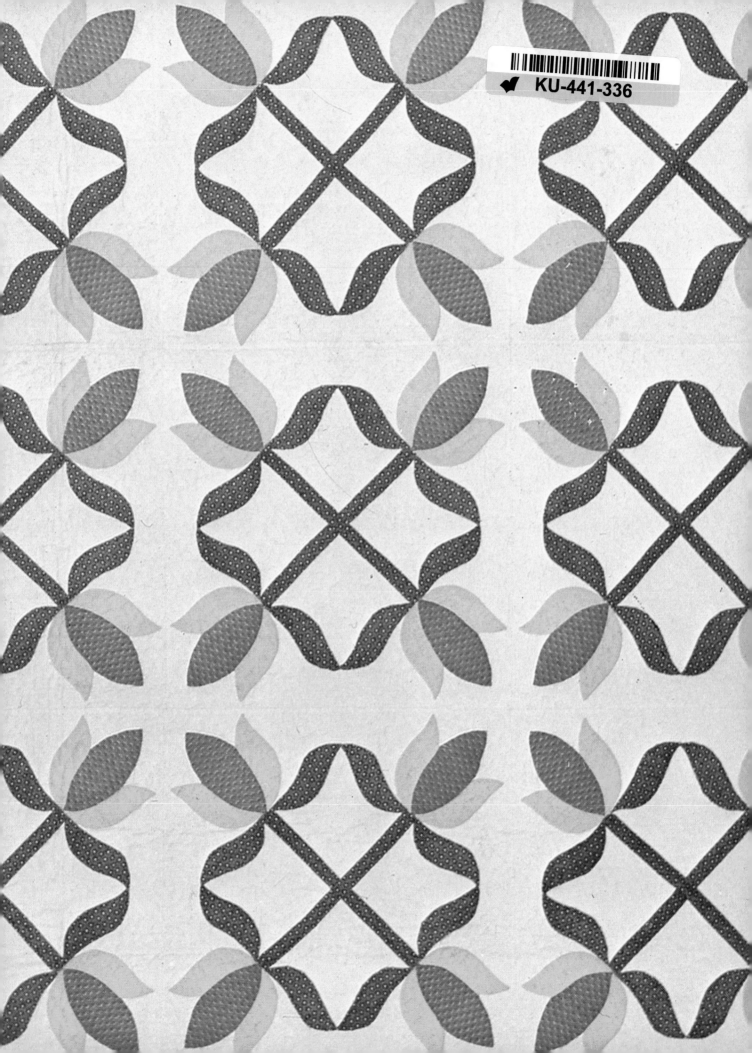

KU-441-336

# Decorating with Flowers

## Jill Mackley

Albany Books

Designed and produced by
Albany Books
36 Park Street London W1Y 4DE

First published 1979

Published by Albany Books

Copyright © Albany Books 1979

Printed in Hong Kong

All rights reserved. No part of this
publication may be reproduced, stored
in a retrieval system or transmitted in
any form or by any means, electronic,
mechanical, photocopying, recording or
otherwise, without the prior permission
of the copyright owner

*Picture research: Mary Corcoran*

Pages 4 & 5: *Both the fabric and the carved
wood bear a floral design in this 19th-
century love-seat.* (American Museum,
Bath)

Right: *This* papier maché *dressing table
dates from around 1850. The ornate floral
decoration is inlaid mother-of-pearl.*
(Cooper-Bridgeman)

Endpapers: *American quilt with a tulip
design.* (The American Museum, Bath)

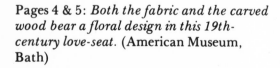

# Contents

# Introduction

The use of flowers as decoration is found from earliest times to the present day. Anyone who is interested will find that museums, art galleries, public buildings and private houses offer examples of all kinds. Flowers in decoration appear, like their counterparts in nature, in the most unexpected places.

The love of flowers, for their bright hues and graceful and varied forms, seems to be a universal taste which reaches far back into history. They are represented in many different ways and many aspects of flowers are revealed.

Among the examples of floral decoration in this book are pieces of jewellery in gold and precious stones, an American quilt made from carefully preserved pieces of chintz, the magnificent tiles of the Topkapi Palace and the bright brushstroke painting of the narrow boat. The treatment of the flowers is quite different in each case which only serves to emphasize the many aspects and endless appeal of flowers.

Flowers are so much part of our lives that designers throughout the world continue to find inspiration from them and from the rich floral traditions of the past.

Right: *Lacquer mirror case and cover, decorated with naturalistic flowers.* (Victoria and Albert Museum, London)

Below left: *Late 18th-century tea caddy and bread basket.* (Cooper-Bridgeman)

Below centre: *Ornate Victorian toilet with a raised oak motif* (Lucinda Lambton)

# Flower Arranging

Flower arranging in the past has varied in style from one culture to another. The Egyptians' use of flowers was simple and orderly. The lotus, which was the sacred flower of the Goddess Isis, appears continually in their art and architecture, and is often shown as a single bloom in a vase.

In China, which has long been known as the 'Flowery Kingdom', early arrangements show a love of nature coupled with the restraint which was part of the religious feeling that permeated life there.

The Greeks and Romans employed professional flower arrangers to make wreaths and garlands. These were given to athletes, poets, civic leaders and victorious soldiers. Garlands were exchanged by lovers, worn at weddings and hung on doors on festive occasions. Roses were very popular but lilies, violets, cornflowers, irises, cyclamen, crocus and various shrubs and aromatic herbs were also used.

The use of roses during festivals in Rome was lavish. The petals were strewn on tables and couches at banquets and sometimes even on the streets. Twelve different varieties are known to have been grown. In a Roman mosaic dating from the 2nd century AD a basket of flowers is shown filled with a charming group of roses and other flowers.

The enormous upsurge of interest in botany and horticulture which occurred in the 17th century can be seen in the Flemish paintings of flower arrangements. In 18th century France the paintings show the soft colours of the flowers and the beauty of the containers, typical of the time.

The Victorians who showed an enormous interest in flowers and plants used rather harsh colour schemes and severely symmetrical arrangements. The

Pages 10-16: *A variety of different arrangements by plantswoman, Valerie Finnis, showing seasonal as well as stylistic combinations.* (Valerie Finnis)

Victorian posy is a typical example. Only the heads of the blooms are visible and they are arranged in concentric circles, usually edged with fern or the striped grass known as 'gardener's garters' and the whole finished off with paper lace and a ribbon.

Symbolism has been connected with flowers for centuries. In Egypt the lotus, which came from the damp regions, was associated with prayers for rain. Early Chinese arrangements often used certain flowers to convey a message to the viewer.

The Victorians attached so many meanings to flowers that messages could be conveyed by particular combinations of different flowers. Many books were produced on the 'language of flowers'.

Today such symbolism is rare except perhaps for white heather which still stands for luck and red roses for love. However, many old superstitions still hold regarding the bringing indoors of certain flowers considered unlucky.

Traditionally, flower arrangements in

*Overleaf, top left:* Spring *flowers in a* tulipière. *These vases for tulips, and other flowers, were made mainly at Delft in the late 17th and early 18th centuries. There are two main kinds — pagoda-shaped and fan-shaped, each with nozzles to hold the flowers. This one is a reproduction in wood and brass.* (Valerie Finnis)

16

the West are of masses of flowers, solid in outline. Although the blooms may not actually touch, the general effect is of tightly packed flowers. Their shapes are revealed against the contrasting colour of neighbouring flowers and leaves rather than by space around each flower. In modern design the beauty of the individual bloom is considered important and the spaces between are an intrinsic part of the design.

In a general way, flower arrangement today can be said to fall into three groups. Firstly, the 'mass', in which a group of flowers and foliage, either all of one kind or of different varieties, colours and textures, are arranged in a more or less traditional manner. The second type

is the 'line' arrangement where the silhouette and the line of movement is stressed. This form of arrangement has come from Japan. The third type of arrangement is a combination of the other two. Strong lines of a design are filled in with flowers and leaves. Often accessories are used with this kind of arrangement as is frequently seen in church flowers where a biblical story or the theme of a festival is illustrated with flowers.

The decoration of churches and cathedrals with flowers is very popular and flower festivals are sometimes held in small village churches while cathedrals can hold larger, international flower festivals.

Far right, top: *Late 16th-century coffer with leaf and flower motif.* (Cooper-Bridgeman)

Far right, bottom: *A 16th-century armchair of carved oak.* (Angelo Hornak)

Right: *The Chapel at Chatsworth House, Derbyshire. Wood carving by Grinling Gibbons.* (British Tourist Authority)

# Grinling Gibbons 1648-1721

Grinling Gibbons stands out as one of the greatest craftsmen of his day. His carvings of flowers, birds and fruit grace many English country houses. He preferred to work in lime wood, a tough, white, smooth grained wood.

His origins remain something of a mystery. It is probable he was of English parentage, but brought up and trained in Holland, where he would have seen

the fine flower painting of the time.

However it was in England that he worked. His talents were recognized while he was still a young man and he was recommended to Charles II. The King commissioned Gibbons to do a considerable amount of ornamental woodwork. His decorations for the State Apartments at Windsor were a great success. Plasterers and carvers in stone and wood began to adopt Gibbons' style of graceful and natural forms. This type of carving required a high degree of technical skill.

Whereas wood carving until this time had tended to copy antique models, Gibbons took his subjects straight from nature. His work is full of flowers, fruit, foliage and birds. There is an attention to detail and a wonderfully realistic touch to his work which is very finely carved. His particular speciality was a hanging festoon of flowers and fruit all carefully copied from nature.

Gibbons worked for Christopher Wren and did some fine work for the Choir of St Paul's Cathedral, London. He decorated the baptismal font in St James's Church, Piccadilly and the chapel at Windsor.

He was the carver most sought after by the great landowners of the day, who were continually adding to and improving their country houses. His work is to be seen at Burleigh, Chatsworth, Petworth and elsewhere.

A vast amount of carving is said to be the work of Grinling Gibbons but he could not possibly have executed it all himself. Much of it was probably done by the numerous carvers whom he employed to carry out his work.

Below: *St James's Church, Piccadilly, London. Wood carving by Grinling Gibbons.* (Cooper-Bridgeman)

# Floral Marquetry

Left: *English cabinet, late 17th-century, with floral marquetry of ivory and mixed woods.* (Cooper-Bridgeman)

In the method of inlaying contrasting materials to form patterns, which is known as marquetry, many different woods were used. The woods were dyed, stained and scorched to produce a variety of colours. Sycamore dyed green was known as harewood and was often used for the foliage in the popular floral designs of the late 17th and 18th centuries. To imitate the shadows on leaves and petals the pieces were dipped into hot sand which darkened the wood.

Apart from wood, expensive materials such as ivory, tortoiseshell, and metals, sometimes silver, were used.

The technique involved in creating complicated floral patterns required great skill. The designs were made up in sections to begin with. Finally, and with great care, they were fitted to each other and into the background.

Two important pieces of furniture often decorated with floral marquetry in the 17th and 18th centuries were the commode, a low chest with drawers, and the cabinet. The tops, fronts and sometimes the ends of commodes were decorated with floral pictures inspired by Dutch paintings. Others had the entire surface covered with designs of flowers, urns and birds.

During his exile, the future King Charles II of England became used to the high standards of design and craftsmanship in France and Holland. On his restoration to the English throne in 1660 he introduced these standards into England. In reaction to the years of Puritan severity, furniture decorated with floral patterns soon became very popular. English furniture around this time copied the work of French and Dutch cabinet makers. These early English pieces often had flowers and leaves set in oval panels, surrounded by decorative borders.

Bouquets of lifelike roses, tulips, daffodils and other flowers appear in vases and tied in bunches with graceful bows and floating ribbons.

Right: *Bureau Mazarin, French c. 1690, decorated with floral marquetry.* (Victoria and Albert Museum, London)

Below left: *A beautiful example of marquetry using sycamore and other woods for this late 19th-century escritoire.* (Angelo Hornak)

Below right: *Another fine example of marquetry using wood and mother-of-pearl inlays.* (Christie's, London)

Below: *This detail from an early 19th-century cabinet is an example of penwork, a technique which imitated marquetry.* (Cooper-Bridgeman)

# Tapestry

Up to the early 14th century ornamental designs of animals and heraldry formed the main subjects of tapestries. During the 14th century designs became more varied. Figure compositions became popular and a growing interest in plants and flowers was reflected in the appearance of flowering plants in the backgrounds.

*Verdure* (or 'green') tapestries which were one of the most common types, were produced in large numbers from the 14th century onwards. In *verdure* tapestries various kinds of leaves, dwarf trees and stylized plants and flowers were used. There is a lively feeling for nature in many of the designs. Animals and flights of birds are often shown emerging

Below: The Renaissance Garden. *Brussels tapestry woven c. 1580. The borders are decorated with figures, fruit and flowers.* (Cooper-Bridgeman)

Bottom: *Gothic Tournai tapestry, showing animals among flowering plants, irises, daisies and strawberries.* (S. E. Franses, London)

from among the bushes and flowers.

An increasing interest in the world of nature is clearly reflected in the careful representation of many different flowering plants. Violets, irises, daisies, dandelions, cornflowers and many others are worked with great charm in refined colours. The trees and flowers of *verdure* tapestries were also used as backgrounds for various subjects and as decorative borders.

Towards the end of the 15th century richly decorative patterns of scattered

flowers often served as backgrounds. Scenes from rural life and the interests and pastimes of the rich were depicted against a field of flowers, usually on a blue or pink ground. These flower strewn tapestries became so numerous that they form a group of their own known as *mille fleurs* (or 'thousand flowers'). A delightful naturalism and a harmonious use of colour is typical of these tapestries. Although *mille fleurs* tapestries were made in considerable numbers not many have survived.

Below: *A Louis XV stool with a contemporary needlework covering.* (Cooper-Bridgeman)

# Tiles

By the end of the 16th century the art of tile making in the Netherlands had reached a high standard which developed into a world-wide trade. The influence of Spain and the contact with Spanish culture had lead to the practice of using tiles as a wall facing.

Vases of flowers appeared at a very early date. They were conventional in design, as painting from life was rare in the decoration of tiles. At first the vases usually contained daisies, later the newly imported tulips became popular. The compositions of these bunches of flowers was so stylized that they became known as *drie tulip* ('three tulip').

Some of the most attractive tiles were those based on arrangements of flowers and fruit — lilies with pomegranites, or tulips with grapes. Their charm lies in the carefully balanced arrangements and the combinations of blue, green and orange.

Tiles decorated with paintings taken from books were quite different. Frans Hals' pupil Judith Leysler made drawings for tulip catalogues. The tile decorators copied these and created tiles with flowers on them which brought into the house a life-like flower image. These tiles have considerable impact not only because of the fine drawing but also because they were painted in many colours in a period when the blue and white tile was the most widely seen.

The custom of standing a vase of flowers in the hearth during the summer probably lead to the creation of flower pieces composed of many tiles. These made very fine fireplace decorations. The influence of the great flower painters can be seen in these flower vase tableaux. They became increasingly popular in Holland during the 18th century when they were used to decorate kitchens and corridors. In many kitchens

Right: *Flower patterned tiles at Isfahan, Iran.* (Spectrum)

Below: *Dutch wall tiles, early 17th-century, decorated with pomegranates, grapes and flowers.* (Victoria and Albert Museum, London)

27.

C.504-1923.

Left: *Flower patterned tiles at the Topkapi Palace, Istanbul.* (Spectrum)

Below: *Flower patterned tiles at Lotfollah Mosque, Isfahan, Iran.* (Spectrum)

Bottom: *Flower patterned tiles at the Topkapi Palace, Istanbul, former residence of the Ottoman Emperors.* (Spectrum)

a vase of blue and white flowers could be found behind the cooking range.

In the same way that the Dutch tile industry developed during Dutch contact with Spanish culture, the Spanish had derived part of their tile tradition from their association with Islamic culture. After the invasion by the Arabs, in 711, of southern Spain and the ensuing Islamic domination, the technical and artistic influences of the East were evident.

Persia is the home of most of the techniques employed in the production of tiles. Ceramic craftsmen moved freely throughout the Islamic world and

traditions from all over Asia came together in one workshop. As a result tiles from different areas may be very similar in design. The Persian rulers and the Sultans of the Ottoman Empire built many mosques, tombs and palaces, which were lavishly decorated with tiles.

The range and variety of the flower designs found in these tiles is enormous. Some of the flowers were stylized and formal, like those in Persian carpets. Tiles from Isnik, near Istanbul, depict lilies, tulips and carnations in many different patterns. Other designs were of branches of flowering plum against a dark blue background.

# Wax and Shells

During the 18th and 19th centuries ladies of quality spent many of their leisure hours making beautiful and elegant objects for the home. Flowers were a particularly popular subject for this fancywork. An amazing diversity of materials was used to make decorations of various kinds. Flowers were modelled in, among other things, wax, wool, seeds, straw, shells and feathers.

The daughters of the house might spend up to ten years making up a basket of wax flowers. Dealers provided sheets of wax, tools, vases and baskets. Large flowers such as roses or clematis might be pulled apart and used as patterns. Other smaller flowers would be cut from dies. On some bouquets nacre (mother of pearl) was sprinkled onto the tips of petals to give the effect of dew glistening among the blooms. Sometimes tiny glass dewdrops were suspended here and there to catch the light. The flowers were arranged in a small basket of spagnum moss or in a vase, mounted on a wooden base, and covered with a glass dome to protect them from the dust.

In the 18th century there was a great vogue for making many petalled flowers from shells and assembling them into bouquets. Sometimes shells of a single colour were used and this created an effect very like porcelain. The shells were held together with putty and the finished bouquet, often in a vase covered with shells of toning colours, was mounted and covered with a glass dome.

Shell hunting for use in fancywork schemes was a popular diversion at the seaside. More unusual shells could be bought from a dealer. 'Rice shells' were particularly sought after. These were tiny shells from the West Indies and were used for making delicate floral hair decorations as well as ornaments for the drawing room.

Left: *Basket of flowers and fruit, English, late 18th century.* (Richard Hall)

Below: *Fine example of wax and feather flowers with glass dewdrops and mother-of-pearl, French, c. 1850.* (Richard Hall)

# American Stencil

Above: *Stencilled bedroom, c. 1830, from Joshua La Salle House, Windham, Connecticut. Not only the walls but most of the furnishings in this room, including the bedspread, are decorated with stencilled patterns.* (The American Museum, Bath)

Left: *Basket of shell-work flowers, English, early Victorian.* (Spectrum)

In Europe stencilled patterns were used mainly between the late 17th and early 19th centuries, on furniture, wallpapers, textiles and as wall decoration in churches.

During this period the settlers in America were beginning to decorate their homes and stencilling was a simple way of bringing colour into dark interiors. The work was done by travelling painters and continued for many years while wallpapers and carpets remained luxuries beyond the reach of most country families.

Stencils were an ideal way of making a repeated pattern for decorative borders which created the effect of carpeting on wooden floors. The same patterns came to be used as borders on plaster walls. In exchange for bed and board and a small wage the travelling artist would rapidly decorate the floors and walls with simple

designs of flowers, leaves and birds in bold colours.

Dry colours were available from an early date. These colours were often mixed with skimmed milk provided by the householder. The colours used by these early painters were, on the whole, lasting. Black, green, yellow, pink and red are most common, on backgrounds of yellow, red, grey and shades of rose.

The same patterns appear in many different areas and the artists obviously exchanged ideas. Some were geometrical, others were copies of the swags and festoons found in French wallpapers. Flowers were always popular and appear over and over again in borders of flowering stems. On broad wall spaces, often divided by stripes, flower sprigs were scattered creating a charming and lighthearted effect. Woven baskets and urns filled with

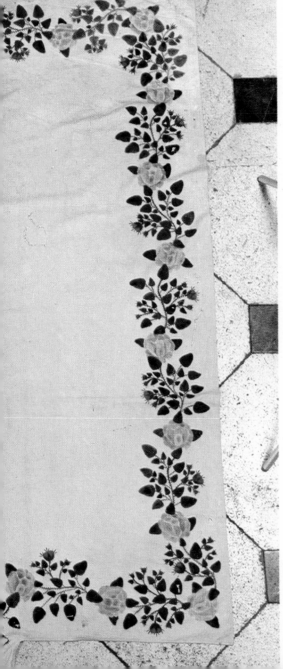

Upper: *Detail of a stencilled wall from Joshua La Salle House, Windham, Connecticut.* (The American Museum, Bath)

Lower: *Bedcover, stencilled with a border of roses and a basket of flowers in the centre.* (The American Museum, Bath)

flowers were popular motifs and are found arranged in various ways.

The flowers of the garden and the meadow bloomed on the walls of these country houses. There were cornflowers, roses, tulips, and many-petalled daisies in sprays and posies. A large number of these stencilled patterns have fallen into disrepair or have been covered up over the years but examples can still be found in museums and private houses.

Stencils were also widely used to decorate furniture of all kinds. Bowls of fruit and vases of flowers often appear in this work. Both subjects were easy to adapt to any shape. Flowers could be massed together or spread out. Roses could be full blown or in bud. Small daisy-like flowers were used to fill in odd corners. Morning Glory was a particular favourite, with its tightly curled buds, open flowers, and flowing tendrils.

The practice of stencilling with gold or bronze powder developed in the United States at a time when the gold ornament on furniture from Europe was greatly admired, but country craftsmen lacked the skills needed to produce elaborate gilt and inlaid metal decoration. In the gold stencil they found a means of meeting the demand for rich detail. The workmanship was frequently very skilled. The flowers were carefully modelled, large blooms were made by overlapping the petal unit many times. The sharpness of line which is typical of stencilled decoration shows up to advantage in the clean outlines of many-petalled flowers.

Whether the gold stencil was first applied to the common chair, on which it is more widely known, or on fine cabinet work, remains uncertain but the chairs were soon increasingly in demand. They were not made of the costly woods found in fine furniture. They were often painted to give a dark background as a contrast to the pale gold of the stencil. Sometimes gold leaf or gold powder was used but in time bronze and other less expensive powders took their place. Furniture decorated with stencilled designs continued to be popular in all parts of the country up to the second half of the 19th century.

# French Paperweights

*Millefiori* is the Italian word, meaning literally 'thousand flowers', which describes the patterns made by using multi-coloured canes of glass seen in cross section. Threads of different coloured glass are drawn out to form canes which are then twisted. When the canes are bunched together and seen in cross section they resemble tiny flowerheads.

This form of decoration was known in ancient Egypt. It continued to develop during Roman times and many beautiful glass bowls decorated with *millefiori* patterns have been unearthed, scattered throughout the far reaches of the Roman Empire.

The use of *millefiori* decorations on glass paperweights is comparatively recent — people have only recently had enough paper work to make a paperweight a useful object. It was in France in the middle of the 19th century that the finest glass paperweights were created. The three main factories involved were Baccarat, St Louis and Clichy. The output from these three firms over a short time was spectacular and their quality has never been surpassed.

## Baccarat

A speciality of the Baccarat factory were weights tightly packed with *millefiori* canes and these were known as 'close' *millefiori* weights. 'Spaced' *millefiori* weights have the canes set well apart on a ground of white filigree which looks like muslin. These particular weights, most of which were produced from 1847 to 1849, are some of the most attractive items from the Baccarat factory. Baccarat also made some weights with the canes arranged in intertwining trefoils which formed a garland. Like other French factories Baccarat made a range of flower weights. The flowers were not realistic; the same leaf pattern was used for all flowers. Several kinds were used, among them cornflowers, primroses and clematis but by far the most popular was the pansy.

Left: *Rocking chair with stencilled and painted decoration of fruit and flowers.* (The American Museum, Bath)

Below: Millefiori *paperweights, French, 19th-century.* (Cooper-Bridgeman)

## St Louis

The weights from this factory were made of the same very clear, heavy, lead glass that was used at Baccarat. The shape was different from the Baccarat weights, being higher domed. The early weights were made in 'close' *millefiori* patterns.

The speciality of St Louis was the so called 'jasper' ground which was made of partly pulverized glass. Some of the most attractive flower weights were on jasper grounds. Various kinds were made. Some were flat bouquets of several *millefiori* flowers grouped together with leaves on a jasper or coloured ground with a border of *millefiori* canes. Others were of single flowers often on a lattice of swirled white or pink opaque glass. The pansy was a favourite flower. Among others were clematis, geranium, fuchsia and dahlia.

The colours at St Louis are delicate, with soft combinations such as pink and pale blue, white and yellow. Most of the best weights made here were produced within a six-year period. From 1850 St Louis seems to have stopped making paperweights.

## Clichy

Neither Baccarat nor St Louis took part in the Exposition of 1844 and Clichy took the main prize in the glass-making section.

The glass at Clichy is clear but not as heavy as that produced by the other two factories. About a third of the weights made at Clichy have a small floret in them which is known as the Clichy rose. The factory was famous for its garland weights. They were made in great variety with endless combinations of loops and circles. The Clichy rose is found in swirl paperweights with contrasting bands of white with pink or purple stripes.

The ever popular pansy weights were made in great numbers, and a few weights feature other flowers which are difficult to identify.

In an age when floral motifs appeared endlessly and on many occasions most unattractively, the French glasshouses provided a product of refreshing beauty.

Above left: *Paperweight, French, 19th-century. Single purple flower.* (Cooper-Bridgeman)

Left: *Flower paperweights, French. The bottom one is an extremely rare Crown Imperial by Baccarat.* (Cooper-Bridgeman)

Right: *Flower paperweights, French, 19th-century.* (Cooper-Bridgeman)

# Well Dressing

Left: *Well dressing at Tissington, Derbyshire. 'David and Goliath'.* (Spectrum)

Below: *Well dressing at Wirksworth, Derbyshire. 'Is your Lord able to deliver you from the lions?'* (Spectrum)

Customs and traditions connected with flowers are as old as man himself. Some are connected with funeral rites, for example the floral necklaces worn by the mourners at the funeral banquet of Tutankhamen and left with other ritual objects in the tomb. Some perpetuate a national or religious event. Others are an act of thanksgiving as in the case of well dressing in the English county of Derbyshire.

It is possible that well dressing has its roots in the Roman custom of venerating water, and that it was introduced to Britain by the occupying Roman forces.

The custom of garlanding wells with chaplets of flowers, particularly wells believed to have healing powers, was once quite common. The present development of well dressing can be traced to the village of Tissington where the ceremony has been observed on Ascension Day for several centuries. According to tradition, the custom was revived during the 17th century as an act of thanksgiving either that the village escaped infection during an epidemic of the plague or for the fact that the wells did not dry up during a drought. Other villages in the area have well dressings during the year. There is one at Eyam, a village that isolated itself during an outbreak of plague in an attempt to prevent the infection spreading. The

1971

AND A LITTLE CHILD

SHALL LEAD THEM

THIS IS MY BELOVED SON

ST. MATTHEW IV

Left: *Well dressing at Ashford-in-the-Water, Derbyshire. 'And a little child shall lead them'.* (Spectrum)

Below left: *Well dressing at Tissington, Derbyshire. 'This is my beloved Son'* (Spectrum)

dressing here combines with a plague commemoration service.

Originally the wells were simply dressed with bunches of flowers and garlands. Then geometrical patterns were introduced, often incorporating a vase or a fountain. Eventually biblical scenes became popular and continue so today.

The method of construction is quite elaborate. Several wooden screens provide the foundation. These screens are studded with nails and then covered with wet clay. Lengths of lining paper marked with the design are then placed on the screens and the design is pricked through. After the paper is peeled away the outline is made with rice, beans, and seeds. Next long-lasting materials such as moss, and leaves are pressed into place. Finally the flower petals are arranged, overlapping each other like scales. According to the strictest traditions of well dressing the flowers which are used must have been grown in the gardens, hedgerows, fields and woods.

# Boats and Caravans

The narrow boats of the English canals were built to pass through the narrow locks of the Midlands, which were built mainly between 1780 and 1840. In the early days the wages were high enough for the captain, who was employed for each boat, to pay a mate, but by 1800 there was a small but growing number of wives working aboard to save the expense of a paid crew. The women having given up their homes ashore set about making their new homes as attractive as possible. Though space was limited, professional painters were employed to decorate everything, inside and out.

The decoration was of two types; bold designs of hearts, diamonds, clubs and crescents, and the so called 'roses and castles'. The boatmen had a love of bright colours, light against dark, which made the paintwork on the bows and cabin sides bright and strong but never gaudy.

The inside of the cabin was small and carefully planned. The entrance doors opened outwards and as they were often on show were usually lavishly decorated.

Above: *Canal boat painting showing diamonds and roses.* (Spectrum)

Just inside the doors stood the stove and beyond that a tall cupboard known as the 'table cupboard' as the top half hinged down to form a table. This was usually decorated with castles and roses. Another tall cupboard hinged down to form a bridge with a seat opposite and this was the bed.

The cupboards and drawers were made with centre panels which were easy to decorate. First everything would be given a coat of light varnish and combed to give a wood grain appearance. Then the doors, drawers and all moveable pieces of cabin equipment were decorated.

The inside of a cabin would usually be decorated in a day and the brushstrokes were simple and decisive. Some painters used a variety of flowers, but the most important were roses. The roses were first painted as discs surrounded by

Right: *Restored Romany caravan.* (Spectrum)

Below: *Canal boat painting. Jug and handbowl decorated with stripes and roses.* (Spectrum)

44

green leaves. The petals, in a lighter colour, were then brushed in with a single stroke. Then lighter highlights and the veining on the leaves were added. Some painters also used a mass of daisy-like flowers consisting of many brushstroke petals on a blue disc.

Not only the exterior of the boat and the fitted cupboards and drawers were painted but also objects such as handbowls, water cans and stools. When everything was put together the effect in the confined space of the cabin was stunning.

A similarly bright and colourful form of decoration is found on Romany caravans. There is a belief that there is a connection between the boatmen and the Gypsies. It is thought that some Gypsies who worked as labourers on the canals stayed on as boatmen when the canals were completed. Whether this is so or not, the style of painting found on the Romany wagon is quite unlike the naturalistic work found on the narrow boats. Most of the decoration on wagons is of painted and carved patterns of curving scrollwork and stylized leaves and flowers. Sometimes birds are introduced, but the only realistic painting is of horses, which are an important part of Gypsy culture.

Right: *Meissen porcelain vase, c. 1725, decorated in an oriental style with the rich colours which mark some early master-pieces of the Meissen factory.* (Cooper-Bridgeman)

Below: *Detail of a restored Romany caravan showing the realistic painting of horses' heads.* (Spectrum)

# Porcelain

Porcelain was made in China as early as the 7th or 8th century AD. In Europe the process was first used at Meissen in 1709 and from there it spread throughout the West. The passion for porcelain affected the whole of Europe during the 18th century.

Flowers have always been a popular theme for the decoration of fine china. The delicate and luminous quality of the material seems particularly suited to the graceful forms and varied hues of flowering plants. Prints formed the basis of almost every kind of porcelain decoration although some of the simpler flower designs were copied from patterns specially painted in water colours.

At Meissen the first flowers were painted in a formal oriental manner. The characteristic 'German flowers' were to appear in about 1740. These were painted with great botanical accuracy and were based on coloured engravings from botanical books. Each flower was painted singly with a cast shadow round it. Often a bee or a butterfly hovered above the bloom. Among the early examples of this flower-and-insect design is a complete service painted for the Elector Clemens August of Cologne.

This style of flower painting was taken up at Chelsea, London, where it soon developed into a freer style in the soft beautiful colours typical of the Chelsea 'red anchor' period. Much of the painting was taken from a book about the botanical gardens established in Chelsea by Sir Hans Sloane.

The importance of Meissen as the centre of porcelain manufacture in Europe was badly affected by the Seven Years' War. In 1756 Dresden was occupied by Prussian troops, the kilns were destroyed and many of the workers dispersed.

Shortly after the process of porcelain making was discovered at Meissen, modellers began to compete with each other in displaying the beauty of the material. The factory at Vincennes became famous for its exquisite porcelain flowers. Forty-six girls were employed to model lilies, roses, carnations and other flowers. These

Top right: *Chelsea Botanical plates, 18th-century. The shadows of the insects give a feeling of naturalism.* (Cooper-Bridgeman)

Right: *A pair of Meissen coral-ground vases decorated with Indianische Blumen (used on Meissen porcelain from the 1720s.)* (Cooper-Bridgeman)

Far right: *Meissen porcelain coffee pot and cover, c. 1740-50, with flowers painted in enamel colours and with gilt decoration.* (Cooper-Bridgeman)

flowers were used to decorate clocks and gilded sconces. Sometimes they were twisted round the metal branches of candelabra or used to form a trellis of flowers behind groups of china figures. Others were mounted on wire stems and placed in vases.

Madame de Pompadour, the mistress of Louis XV, received the King in her winter garden which had been filled with four hundred and fifty porcelain flowers, each one perfumed with its own scent. It is said that the King was deceived into thinking that the flowers were real!

In 1753 the factory was taken under royal protection at the suggestion of Madame de Pompadour, and in 1756 it was moved to Sèvres and became the property of the King.

The Royal French factory at Sèvres took over the role that Meissen had held as the leader of fashion in porcelain making. A most distinctive style developed with rich strong colours, lavish gilding and fine painting. Flowers, more delicate than the German

ones, were a main decorative feature. They appeared in sprays, and light and delicate garlands.

Many artists were employed at Sèvres. The rules were very strict and a painter who specialized in flower painting was not allowed to paint anything but flowers. Workers were not encouraged to take their skills to other factories and flight was punished by imprisonment.

The French Revolution put an end to the production of such luxuries for a time, although the factory was saved from destruction by the National Assembly which decided in 1791 to make it the common property of the citizens of France.

In the second half of the 18th century the earlier exuberant style of decoration became more reserved and classical. Sprays of flowers were replaced by neat posies in baskets and regular borders of floral garlands.

During the Napoleonic era flowers were often shown growing from the earth, massed in baskets, or as flowerets arranged in initials. Sometimes flowers

Left: *Chelsea Botanical circular soup-tureen.* (Cooper-Bridgeman)

Below: *Royal Meissen porcelain, enamel and ormolu centrepiece supplied to the Court of Augustus III of Saxony.* (Cooper-Bridgeman)

were arranged to convey a cryptic message, where the initial letters of the flower names spell out a word or a name.

In the late 18th century, flowers of all kinds are found in the decoration of porcelain. One example is the 'Flora Danica' service made at the Royal Copenhagen factory. This was started about 1790 and was intended for the Empress Catherine III of Russia. There are over sixteen hundred pieces. Each piece was painted with botanical specimens taken from a book, published in Copenhagen, which illustrated in scientific detail the plants and flowers of Denmark.

In the first quarter of the 19th century the use of flowers in porcelain decoration was given a new lease of life by the work of the English painter William Billingsley. The bouquets and borders in his work portray the flowers found in English country gardens. He was particularly fond of a full blown rose. His flowers were painted naturalistically and the highlights on the petals were wiped out with a brush. His style proved very popular and was quickly taken up at other English factories.

Left: *A pair of Mennecy ormolu-mounted figures and flowers.* (Cooper-Bridgeman)

Below: *Mennecy porcelain* sucrier *and cover,* c. *1755, decorated with naturalistically painted flowers.* (Cooper-Bridgeman)

Left: *Coalport cup and saucer, c. 1810.* (Cooper-Bridgeman)

Below: *Coalport vase, painted and decorated with applied flowers.* (Michael Holford)

# Persian Carpets

The carpets and rugs of Persia (present-day Iran) have long been regarded as the finest from the Orient. They were manufactured in antiquity and many of the oldest surviving date from the 16th and 17th centuries. The Persian carpet designer achieved a harmony of design and colour which is admired throughout the world.

The carpets are made from the hard wearing wool of the sheep from the highlands of Persia. The dyes used by the weavers were, until recently obtained from plants. Madder, which grows wild, yields red, indigo is cultivated for its blue dye, ripe turmeric gives green, and brown comes from bark and from walnut shells. Some colours come from animal sources — sheep's blood and the crushed shells of insects.

In general the Islamic passion for geometric patterns is not so obvious in Persian carpets. Instead there are a number of ornaments taken from nature. These are mainly curling tendrils and flower motifs. Among the shapes inspired by flowers are 'palmettes' and 'rosettes'. Palmettes are large flowers seen as though cut in half. Rosettes are arrangements of flower petals arranged symmetrically round a central point. The tendrils bear buds and leaves as well as the various rosettes and palmettes. A variety of flowers are found in different designs: pinks, tulips, roses and hyacinths, all in very stylized forms.

In the 18th and early 19th centuries a design known as the 'garden' carpet was particularly popular. It represented a formal Persian garden, with flower beds, paths, streams, fishponds and birds. The same nostalgic feeling for flowers is found in the so called 'vase' carpets. These are longish, narrow carpets decorated with various flowers. Among the flowers are one or two hidden vases. During the long winter months these flowery carpets are a beautiful substitute for a garden.

Below: *Persian vase carpet, 16th- to 17th-century.* (Cooper-Bridgeman)

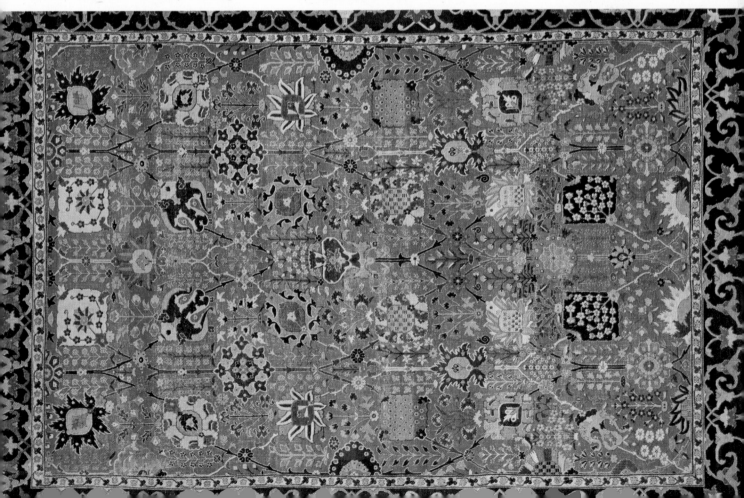

# Glass

Glass is one of the most remarkable substances known to man. It can be made as colourless as water, as opaque as china, or tinted with all the colours of the rainbow. While hot it can be blown or moulded into a variety of shapes. The graceful forms and varied colouring of flowers have appeared in the design and decoration of glass from earliest times.

Glass for making objects such as beads seems to have appeared about 3000 BC. Glass vessels appear later, around 1500 BC. A glass beaker shaped like a lotus bud was found in the tomb of an Egyptian Pharoah. The glass has been shaped by moulding on a clay core. In parts of Syria and Mesopotamia solid blocks of greenish glass occurred, which were hollowed out and shaped by abrasion into dishes with petal shaped decorations.

Much prized in Roman times were flat *millefiori* bowls. These had floral decorations formed by coloured glass canes seen in cross section. The ill-fated Cleopatra had a collection of them which were sold by the Emperor Augustus.

The discovery that glass, while hot, could be blown into different shapes revolutionized glass-making and from this time, around 100 BC, until the fall of the Roman Empire, glass of all kinds was made throughout Italy and the Roman colonies. With the fall of the Empire the art of glass-making died out in Europe but continued in the East. By the 13th and 14th centuries there was a distinctive Islamic style of enamelling and gilding. As the use of solid gold was forbidden on religious grounds the mosque lamps were decorated with lavish gold painting, the coloured borders often showing trefoils and lotus flowers.

Some beautiful flower decorations are found in the glass from the Royal Factory of La Granja de San Ildefonso in

Left: *Persian Rose ground vase carpet.* (Michael Holford)

Below: *Spanish glass from La Granja de San Ildefonso, 18th-century. Covered jar decorated with gold flowers.* (Cooper-Bridgeman)

*Pages 56 & 57: A variety of Art Nouveau lamps and glassware made around the turn of the century. The stained-glass lamps are known as Tiffany lamps after their designer, Louis Comfort Tiffany; the vases are by Lalique. Note the different interpretations of flowers — naturalistic and more stylized. (Top left: Cooper-Bridgeman; Left and below: Sotheby's, London)*

*Overleaf, left: A love for flowers found its way into the jewellery of the time. (Sotheby's, London)*

*Overleaf, right: Further examples of Art Nouveau glassware. (Sotheby's, London)*

Spain. In the second half of the 18th century the factory used a method of firing gilt onto glass, which lasted extremely well. The painting was done with ground gold leaf mixed with honey. The design was fixed to the surface of the glass by firing at a low temperature. Sometimes it was combined with engraving and some very attractive flower designs were created. The factory also experimented with coloured glass and with enamel painting. The flower painting is very soft and charming. Roses and other garden flowers were painted in pastel shades of pinks, pale greens, blues, yellows and white.

In the 18th century much beautiful naturalistic flower work was done by diamond and wheel engraving. The trade name for tableware decorated in this way was 'flowered glass'. This form of decoration was particularly popular in England and Holland. The English glass-makers had used the Roman technique of adding lead oxide to their glass which produced a clear hard glass ideal for deep cutting and wheel engraving. At first a single flower, a rose, carnation

or daisy might ornament the side of a drinking glass. Later other flowers appeared; a sunflower or a tulip and, on the opposite side of the glass, a butterfly or a bee would be engraved.

Venetian glass of the 18th century made considerable use of floral motifs. The great glass chandeliers were often decorated with opaque glass flowers in brilliant colours. Mirrors, which played such an important part in the glass industry of Venice, were often composed of a profusion of flowers made of pink and white opaque glass.

## Art Nouveau Glass

The style of decoration popular in the 1890s and the early 1900s, known as Art Nouveau was found in all the decorative arts. Some of the finest examples of this style are found in the glass and jewellery of the time.

Art Nouveau was a romantic movement influenced by Japanese art, which was enjoying a vogue in France at the time. The lines which are curving and flowing are all based on natural motifs: flowers, in particular the convolvulus

and nasturtium, and insects.

In France Emile Gallé experimented with opaque and coloured glass decorated with enamels. Gallé was an enthusiastic gardener and botanist. His interest in plant forms was something that he shared with Japanese artists whose work he greatly admired. Using a technique said to have been inspired by Chinese snuff bottles, which were then being imported, he made vases using glass of different colours in many layers. The layers were then cut away, with acid or a grinding tool, in various thicknesses to reveal patterns of flowers and insects. The designs seem to cling round the vases in curving lines.

In the United States Louis Tiffany, a gifted artist, became as internationally well known as Gallé. Tiffany used a technique in which layers of coloured glass ran over each other making a swirling pattern. He called this glass 'favrile' and used gold to make flowing patterns of flowers and feathers. Many Tiffany vases are not only decorated with flowers but are also made in elongated flower shapes.

As electricity became more popular Tiffany designed the lamps, which are perhaps the best-known aspect of his work. These lamps were made with a cast bronze stem in the shape of a stylized plant. The shades were made of pieces of glass set into various flower shapes. The lily and the wisteria were among his most successful models.

# Wallpaper

Until the arrival of paper, wall coverings of decorated leather and painted or woven cloth were used both for warmth and decoration. The Chinese were making paper some time around the 1st century AD, and in the course of time the knowledge spread west to Baghdad, Egypt, Morocco and Spain. It reached Italy, Germany and other parts of Europe during the 11th century.

Wallpapers obviously do not have a very good chance of surviving to the present day, but some papers, particularly those used to line drawers and boxes, have withstood the passage of time.

Some of the earliest papers which have survived are black and white floral designs, very similar to the embroidery known as 'blackwork'. This is a style in which various patterns, often floral, were picked out in black thread. It was particularly popular between 1500 and 1650. In some paper the stitches are reproduced by cross hatching and the paper designer and the embroiderer probably used the same books of patterns. The flowers most commonly used were the favourites of the period: pinks, pansies, columbines and roses.

In the middle of the 17th century Chinese papers began to arrive in Europe (confusingly called 'India' papers because they were brought over in ships of the East India Company). The flowers on these papers were beautifully drawn and meticulously accurate. They were greatly admired and 'India' papers decorated with flowers, shrubs and a powdering of exotic birds and butterflies remained favourites up to the middle of the 18th century. The Chinese made these papers especially for the European market and drew their inspiration from the delightful painted silk hangings which adorned the houses of the wealthy in China.

In the second half of the 17th century French wallpaper makers were producing outstandingly beautiful papers. Some of the most charming were to be found at the Paris factory of the world-famous Réveillon, who produced papers on a large scale. His floral papers were superbly drawn and coloured.

By the early 1800s more and more people were seeking to brighten up their rooms with wallpapers. Manufacturers were trying to develop a machine which would produce a continuous roll of paper for machine printing and in 1840 a cheap machine-printed paper, which was much admired, appeared on the market.

However, by the 1850s the design and colourings of the new machine printed papers were being regarded with disfavour. The critics pointed out that the object of wallpaper was not to make the wall appear as if it had flowers growing on it but rather that the paper should enhance the room as a whole.

Owen Jones was an influential designer at this period and in 1856 he published his 'Grammar of Ornament'. In this book the geometric forms of flowers and plants is stressed, and had a considerable influence on floral wallpaper designs.

## William Morris

William Morris was a designer who showed a far greater feeling for natural forms than was then fashionable. He observed from nature and studied the illustrations in the old herbals. He began producing, among other things, wallpaper. In 1861 he founded a firm with other designers sympathetic to his views. The first paper to be put on the market was 'Daisy', which was the best seller of all his papers. Many of his designs, some with large scale flowers suited to grand rooms and others, like 'Blackthorn' which give the effect of a flowery bower, are still in production today. Morris was a keen observer of nature and his delight in the beauty of flowers and plants is apparent in his designs.

Right: *18th-century Venetian commode with green chinoiserie lacquer.* (Angelo Hornak)

Right: *English 'Blackwork' coif, 16th-century.* (Michael Holford)

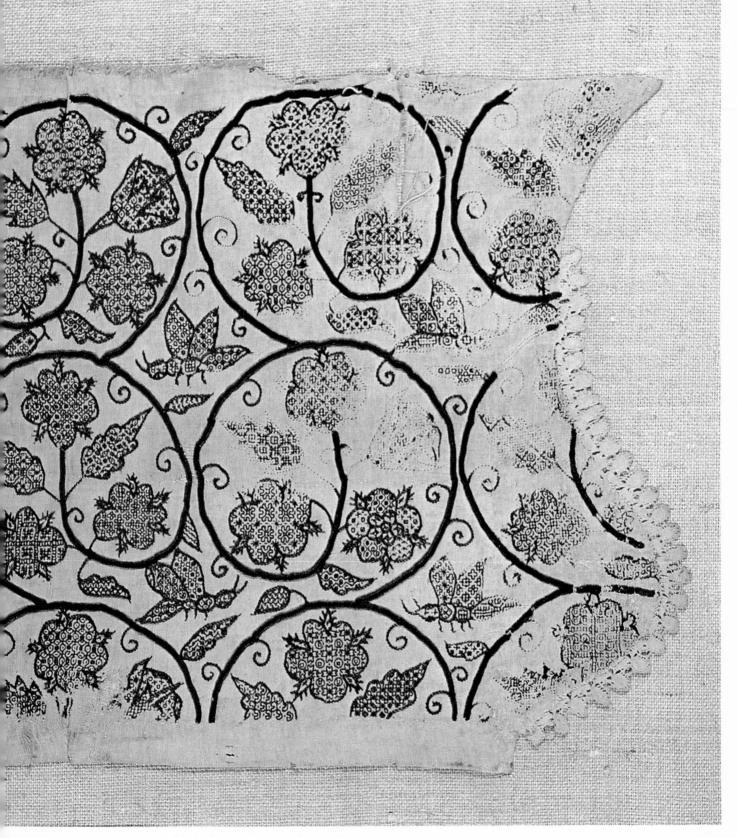

Right: *'Compton' print, designed by William Morris.* (Sanderson Triad)

Far right, top: *William Morris design 'Blackthorn'* (Sanderson Triad)

Far right, bottom: *William Morris chair upholstered in 'Original Bird' woollen tapestry.* (Angelo Hornak)

# Lace

Forms of open mesh or network have been discovered in the tombs of ancient Egypt, and embroidery similar to lace has been made throughout the Middle East for many centuries. The craft spread to Italy and then all over Europe.

There are many different kinds of lace but they all fit into one of three groups, bobbin, needlepoint, and decorated nets.

Bobbin lace is made by plaiting and weaving threads wound round bobbins. The lace is made on a firm pillow. A pricked out pattern is tacked to the pillow and each twist of the bobbin is held in place by a pin. The pattern is formed by more compact weaving than that used in the background mesh. The design is sometimes outlined in a heavier thread.

Needlepoint lace is made by a method which evolved from embroidery on fine linen which was then cut away. Later the linen base was done away with and the whole fabric was made with a needle and thread in various forms of buttonhole stitch. The lace made by this method is very beautiful and longlasting, but it

*Lace collar with floral motifs, and detail.* (R. John Hall)

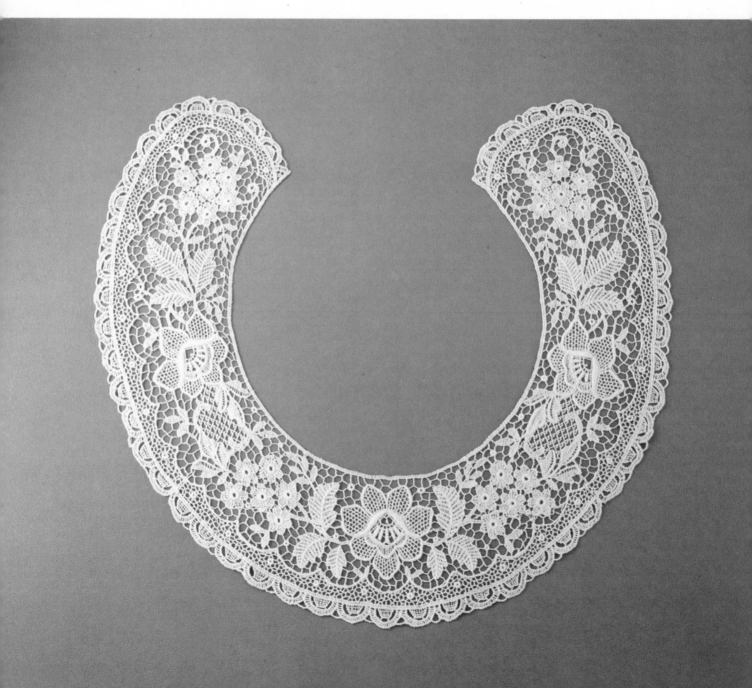

takes longer than other forms of lace work to make.

The third group is the decorated nets. An open mesh, originally made on loom but later by machine, is decorated using a darning stitch.

In all lace designs flowers appear again and again. The flowing lines and shapes of flowers adapt easily to the techniques of lace making. There are many different flowers — roses, carnations, lilies, forget-me-nots, tulips and the wild flowers of the fields and hedgerows.

In different periods the forms of the flowers changed according to fashion. In the 17th century the designs were rich and elaborate and are like the brocades of the time. The skill of the lace makers enabled them to produce flowers with raised edges, sometimes with petals built up on top of each other. The sprays were joined together by elaborate bridges as in *Point de Venise* lace.

Towards the end of the 16th century lace designs had become more ambitious. Early designs had followed simple patterns or the lace makers had used flower forms found in their own gardens. Now the finest draughtsmen in France, Italy and the Low Countries were employed to create beautiful designs. In the 17th and 18th centuries lace became more and more elaborate and a great number of different kinds of lace were made.

# Samplers

Samplers are perhaps the most familiar of old embroideries. From the early 17th century until the middle of the 19th century small girls in Europe and in the countries where Europeans had settled worked on one or more samplers during their school days.

The early sampler, (from *exampler,* a model or pattern to be imitated) was originally used by needlewomen to keep a record of motifs and border designs. Early patterns show various flowers and sprigs in severely geometric designs. The habit of showing a flower or a sprig within a curve, then turning it upside down and repeating it to form a curving border was very popular. It appears time after time in varying forms. These

border patterns were widely used for decorating both personal and household linen.

Although the first pattern book appeared in 1523, and was rapidly followed by many more, samplers continued to be used as before to the end of the 16th century. Samplers of the 16th century are rare now, but those of the 17th are more numerous. These were usually long and narrow in shape. With the exception of those worked with all over patterns, the most lively and colourful are the 'spot' samplers. The motifs of these were often flowers. Roses, pansies, pinks and daisies are easy to recognize and there are other flower shapes more difficult to identify. They were often

worked with silver thread and softly shaded to give a feeling of depth.

The samplers of the 17th century were usually carefully done and often signed and dated. But as printed patterns and embroidery canvas with the design already printed on, became more available, the sampler ceased to be used by needlewomen and became the school-girls' task. Samplers from the late 17th century onwards were often quite out of touch with contemporary styles of needlework. The flowers, which con-tinued to appear, have a stiff old-fashioned look. There may be a pot with a single tulip, a vase with three flowers or a basket with a rose and some care-fully arranged leaves. The looping borders continue with little flowers or buds. Some of the samplers done in America show more liveliness and variety and have flowers which look as if they have been drawn from life. However individual style was unusual and the flowers tend to be traditional in form and arrangement.

Above: *Sampler from Nuremburg, early 18th-century, showing a variety of flowers — in a vase, a posy, a wreath and in borders.* (Cooper-Bridgeman)

Left: *English sampler showing Crystal Palace surrounded by a border of roses and thistles and the date, 1851.* (Michael Holford)

# Pennsylvania German

In 1683 groups of German and Swiss settlers began to arrive in Eastern Pennsylvania, forming one of the first groups of non-English colonists in North America. These people spoke German and are often called Pennsylvania Dutch (*Deutsch,* Anglicized to Dutch). These simple and industrious people brought with them the decorative traditions of their homelands. They were fond of brightly painted flowers, especially the tulip, trees of life, hearts, birds, leaves and geometric designs. These decorations which appear in all Pennsylvania German art come from early German folk art and originally the motifs had a symbolic meaning.

The tulip, which appears everywhere, is a reminder of tulipomania which swept through Europe and particularly Holland in the 17th century. The tulip was also looked upon as a version of the holy lily, its three petals standing for the Trinity.

Decorative flowers are found in profusion in the borders of fractur work. (Fractur is a script based on the calligraphy of medieval manuscripts.) Long after it had died out in Europe fractur writing flourished in America and developed into a splendidly decorative folk art. For generations schoolmasters and ministers made fractur work certificates of birth, baptism, marriage and death. Later the work was done by travelling fractur artists. The lettering gradually gave way to the decorations of ink and watercolours. Flowers appear in endless combinations of tulips, pinks, daisies and roses, in borders, baskets and urns.

Tinware was made and decorated in enormous quantities in Pennsylvania in the first half of the 19th century and became popularly known as 'Pennsylvania tin.' The colours were bright and the designs simple.

The country tinsmith decorated his tinware with brushstroke painting, which all apprentices learned. Most leaves were made with a single brushstroke, a flower by several strokes. The background was usually black or dark brown with decorations in white, yellow, blue and red. The style was dictated by the brushstroke method and the most common decorations were abstract patterns of flowers, fruit and leaves.

Right: *American quilt with a tulip design.* (The American Museum, Bath)

Below: *Dower chest in pine with brightly painted flowers. Made in Jonestown, Pennsylvania by Christian Seltzer, dated 1784.* (Cooper-Bridgeman)

# Knot Gardens

In a medieval garden the beds of herbs were divided into rectangles. As these divisions became more numerous it became fashionable to make them in a decorative way by outlining the beds with low growing shrubs such as thyme, hyssop, lavender and later box. Box had been used many centuries earlier by the Romans to border paths and flower beds.

In France the squared designs were replaced with interlacing ribbon patterns known as *parterre de broderie*. These designs bore a close affinity to the floral embroidery of the time. One gardener, Jean Robin, planted *broderies* of exotic flowers with the idea of supplying the embroiderers with new themes for their work. In France the hedges became more important than the flowers as in the great scrolled designs at Versailles and Vaux-le-Vicomte.

In England these gardens of little hedges filled with flowers were known as 'knots', the English word for *broderie*. Where flowers filled the spaces they were called 'closed knots'. If, however, the spaces were filled with sand, brick or simply paths of grass they were known as 'open knots'.

The flowers in knot gardens tended to be in bloom only during the summer months but the hedges had the advantage of remaining green and attractive throughout the year. The English brought their wild flowers such as primroses, daisies and violets into cultivation.

In addition, plants from the Continent became garden favourites: larkspur, pot marigold, hollyhock and pansy. It was an age of exploration and change which was reflected in the gardening as many plants were introduced from one country to another.

The knot garden in Elizabethan England was an elaborate carpet garden of interwoven hedges and beds of flowers. It is a type of gardening which is still seen today in the form of carpet bedding in parks and the floral clocks and patterns popular in some seaside towns.

*Elizabethan knot garden at New Place, Stratford-on-Avon, edged with box and filled with summer bedding plants.*
(Spectrum)

*Replica knot garden at New Place, Stratford-on-Avon, edged with box and filled with spring flowers. (Spectrum)*

# Jewellery

Jewellery has been made and worn since earliest times. We owe our knowledge of early work to the discoveries of archaeologists, particularly from tombs. Much of the material which has survived is gold. Bronze Age treasure found in the Aegean includes pieces of gold embossed with flower patterns. The gold and silver funeral wreaths of the Greeks often included flowers among the leaves. The floral motif found in ancient jewellery appears throughout the history of European jewellery.

It was in the Renaissance period that the flower became overwhelmingly popular in jewellery design. The interest in natural forms at this time was echoed in the jeweller's treatment of flowers.

Throughout the 17th century, the flower was the principal motif in jewellery design. Its decorative value became so established that it has remained a favourite of European jewellers to this day. Shortly before the middle of the century a passion for the tulip swept Holland. This craze, known as tulipomania, gave a further boost to the popularity of floral themes. Tulips appear in much enamelled and engraved work. The influence of the Dutch flower painters was strong at this time and is reflected in the realistic way in which the flowers are shown.

A favourite jewellers' device during the 17th century were long chains made of linked flowerheads. Some were composed of flowers such as roses or daisies, enamelled in white. Others were made up of large petalled star-like flowers enamelled and inlaid with gold. Often the centre of the flower would be set with a gemstone.

Another example of the 17th century fondness for floral devices is the *giardinetti* ring. The central ornament was in the shape of a garland or a spray of flowers which was set with small coloured stones. Rings in which the whole circlet was enamelled with floral patterns were also very popular.

In the 18th century the Dutch

*Jewellery from Midea, 1425-1400 BC, necklace with flower motif.* (Cooper-Bridgeman)

influence which had played a large part
in the popularizing of floral motifs,
declined. The French were the leaders of
Europe and the formal classical style was
in vogue. The flowers were very simple,
frequently of diamonds, with a single
stone centre without stem or leaves.
They were usually set against a background of scrolled foliage.

After Captain Cook's expedition to
Australia and the South Seas a wave of
enthusiasm for botany swept into the
design of jewellery. Flowers began to
look real, with the correct leaves and
textured stems. Bouquet brooches were
popular, tied with a ribbon and with an
insect, a dragonfly or butterfly on a
hidden wire so that it trembled in the air
above the flowers.

At the beginning of the 18th century
the flowers were flat and formal. Later
they were made as realistic as possible
with the *tremblant* insect adding a final
lifelike touch. During this period designs
were often made in sections so that a
piece consisting of several large flowers
could be taken apart to form a set
consisting of a brooch with matching
ear-rings.

Around 1825 the French used an
effect known as *pampilles* (waterfalls)
and this was quickly taken up by the
English. Each segment hung on articu-
lated wire so that the jewels hanging
there swung and sparkled indepen-
dently. The pendulous flowers of the
fuchsia were well suited to this
technique.

The flower motif was never more
popular than during the Victorian era.
The taste for invention coupled with
sentimentality led to an outburst of
flowery jewellery and trinkets. Flowers
appeared as garlands, enamelled and set
with stones, in posies and as single
blooms. Single flowers were popular,
particularly sweet peas, roses and convolvulus, the last a favourite of Prince
Albert. There were complete bouquets
of flowers with the leaves and stems
enamelled to make them look real.
Diamonds were used to give a dewy
glitter and very often a *tremblant* bee or
butterfly hovered above minutely copied
and sculpted from nature.

8745

8748

8744

Pages 78 & 79: *Woman's gold jewellery from Midea, 1400 BC, showing a simple daisy-like flower motif.* (Cooper-Bridgeman)

Page 82: *Diamond necklace, c. 1760, in a stylized flower and leaf pattern.* (Cooper-Bridgeman)

Page 83: *Victorian mosaic brooch, c. 1850.* (Michael Holford)

Left: *The Cheapside Hoard. In 1912 a workman digging on a site in the City of London found a box containing about 230 items, which had probably been buried before the Great Fire in 1666. The variety of colour, both in gemstones and enamels, is typical of the late Elizabethan era.* (Cooper-Bridgeman)

## Art Nouveau Jewellery

The flowers found in Art Nouveau jewellery are often not the usual flowers associated with European jewellery design. The strong Japanese influence found in Art Nouveau led designers to look at the kinds of flowers found in Japanese art. The ragged petalled chrysanthemum and the iris appear, and plants with trailing habit and curling tendril.

The designs of Art Nouveau jewellery were strange and sensuous and there is often an underlying somewhat sinister feeling about many pieces. The movement as a whole did not enjoy a wide popularity and only lasted from about 1895 until the First World War.

In the main, it was in France that this style of jewellery was made and worn. Among the most well known of the designers working there were René Lalique and Georges Fouquet. Insects were used a great deal both with flowers and on their own. In a brooch by Georges Fouquet, made in enamelled gold, a bee sucks nectar from a flower. In a hatpin by René Lalique a sunflower of carved opal has five black and gold wasps surrounding it and sucking the nectar. The strange shapes of orchids attracted designers and there is a comb in ivory and horn and an orchid brooch by Georges Fouquet which display the curious form of this exotic flower. Enamelling was of great importance in this jewellery. In France enamels were often set in a metal framework, giving a stained-glass effect.

As the movement progressed, bright enamels gave way to paler colours. Silver rather than gold was used and the stones were pale; opals and moonstones appear often. Coloured glass engraved with flowers and insects became popular and is often seen in Lalique's work.

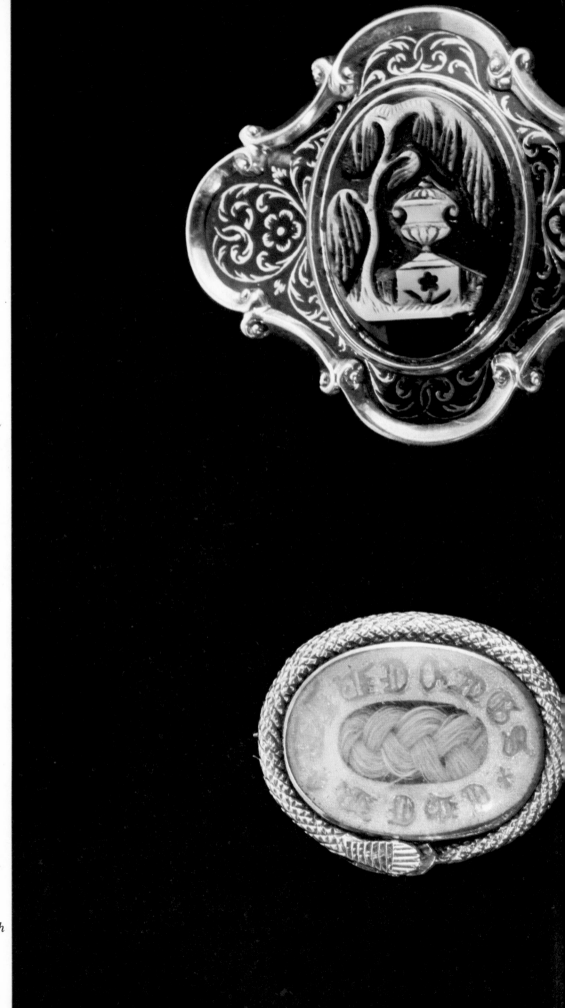

*Mourning brooch, mid-Victorian, set in gold with a flower motif in pearls.* (Cooper-Bridgeman)

# Flower Prints

Left: *Tulips, with the flat fields of Holland and a windmill in the background, from* The Temple of Flora *published by Robert Thornton.* (Cooper-Bridgeman)

Below: *Loudon's* Ladies Flower Garden. Ornamental Plants, *published in 1840.* (NHPA, L. H. Newman)

Below right: *Loudon's* Ladies Flower Garden. Lilies, *published in 1841.* (NHPA, L. H. Newman)

By the early 18th century the art of wood engraving had declined and was taken over by engraving on metal. There were botanical advantages in this method as fine detail is more possible when incised on metal.

Volumes with fine engraved plates tended to become picture books where the text was reduced to a minimum. This kind of book appealed more to the wealthy amateur than to the serious botanist. The florilegeum was a flower book designed to show the decorative possibilities of flowers arranged in vases. In contrast to the herbals which described useful garden plants, the florilegeum displayed flowers for their beauty. Many such books were commissioned by wealthy patrons.

In 1730 an enterprising grower, Robert Furber, brought out what was in effect the first English seed catalogue. It was called *Twelve Months of Flowers* and showed the flowers which bloom each month, 'coloured to life' and grouped in a bowl. Each flower was numbered and a key given below.

*The Temple of Flora* is part of an ambitious publication undertaken for Robert Thornton. He commissioned various artists to make paintings for engraving. To each plate Thornton added his own description of the flowers. Each species was painted in an appropriate setting, so that tulips appear against a background of flat Dutch fields.

Much of the work of 18th century

botanical illustrators was connected with the work that appeared after Charles Linnaeus issued his new principles of plant classification.

George Ehret who was born in Heidelberg in 1704 worked largely in England where he met Sir Hans Sloane and other gardeners and botanists. After visiting Linnaeus in Holland he returned to England where the patronage of botanical gardening was at its height. He produced many beautiful paintings and sometimes engraved his own work for publication. Among his principal published drawings are those for *Plantae et Papilliones Rariores*.

Interest in flowers was no longer confined to the botanist or herbalist, and books of flower prints proliferated.

Paris was becoming the centre for European painting and among the artists drawn there was Gerard van Spaendonck. He was a fine botanical draughtsman and painter and was master to Pierre Joseph Redouté. Under the patronage of French rulers Redouté established a worldwide reputation. He was the official flower artist of the Empress Josephine who grew many flowers in her gardens at Malmaison. Redouté made over a thousand paintings of roses and produced eight volumes of lily portraits.

Porcelain, tapestry and silk were created with the help of the great flower illustrators. Improved engraving techniques led to the production of superb flower books and prints.

Page 89: *A selection of rose prints by Pierre-Joseph Redouté.* (Spectrum)

Left: *Loudon's* Ladies Flower Garden. *Ornamental Greenhouse Plants, published in 1848.* (NHPA, L. H. Newman)

Below: Favourite Flowers, *Edward Step.* Pyrethrum roseum, *published in 1896.* (NHPA, L. H. Newman)

# American Coverlets

Some of the most outstanding examples of American needlework are to be seen in the imaginative decoration of the many types of bed covers. The typical liveliness of American work and the universal fondness for flower motifs among needlewomen can be seen.

In general it was the policy of the British government to encourage the production of raw materials in its colonies but to discourage industrial development. In a period when textiles were scarce and expensive they became particularly valuable in America. Pieces of rich patterned fabrics, too precious to throw away, were used instead of embroidery. The floral motifs from worn out pieces of India chintz were cut out and stitched onto a plain ground of white linen or cotton. The whole was

then lined and filled with wool or cotton and held in place with a running stitch. This stitching often followed elaborate patterns, many of them floral.

At the time of the American War of Independence the shortage of fabric became even more acute, and from then until the late 1800s patchwork quilts were frequently made.

In America it became the practice for unmarried girls to make thirteen patchwork quilts, often with the help of family and friends. The first quilts which a young girl made would be based on a pattern of squares. As she developed more skill with the needle she would attempt more complicated designs.

Patterns were handed down from mother to daughter and circulated from one household to another. Many of these

Left: *'Flowers in a Vase'*, *a fine flower painting by Jan van Huysum, (1682-1749). The elegant composition and soft colours are in keeping with the French taste in decor of the time.* (Victoria and Albert Museum, London)

Below: *American quilt, chintz.* (The American Museum, Bath)

Overleaf: *American quilt, Rose of Sharon.* (The American Museum, Bath)

designs were based on flowers. The rose was particularly popular with quilt makers. It appears in many patterns, in wreaths, flowers and buds, combined with other flowers and in geometrical forms. The rose appears time and time again in the old quilt names; Mexican Rose, Whig Rose, Rambler Rose, Colonial Rose, and many others.

Many different flowers appear in quilt designs. Among the most popular were sunflowers, cactus flowers, lilies and tulips. Pennsylvania quilts often have tulip designs. It is one of the most common motifs used by the Pennsylvania German communities and was brought with them from the German speaking lands of Europe. It has the advantage of a simple shape which can be managed even by an inexperienced needlewoman. Apart from designs where a flower appears as a single motif, flowers are shown in baskets, in vases, in sprays and posies, and in horns of plenty which were very popular in America.

Patterns moved across the country as people moved on to populate new frontier areas. The names of some changed as they went. The flower motif known as the Meadow Lily in New England became the Prairie Lily west of the Mississippi, and the Mariposa Lily beyond the Rockies.

In many quilts the pattern is made up of identical motifs repeated many times. In others such as Album Quilts the blocks are all different. In an Album Quilt the different blocks are made up by family and friends, usually to mark a special occasion. Often each block has the name of the donor written on it in ink. Flowers were a favourite subject for many Album Quilts, and they appear in all the usual forms. Some in wreaths, some in bunches, baskets or vases, others in geometrical patterns. The finished effect when they are all put together is often very pleasing.

In Baltimore many fine examples of Album Quilts were made and they are often referred to as Baltimore Brides' Quilts. A quilt for a bride usually included hearts in the design. Hearts are not found in any other quilts, being considered unlucky except for a bride.

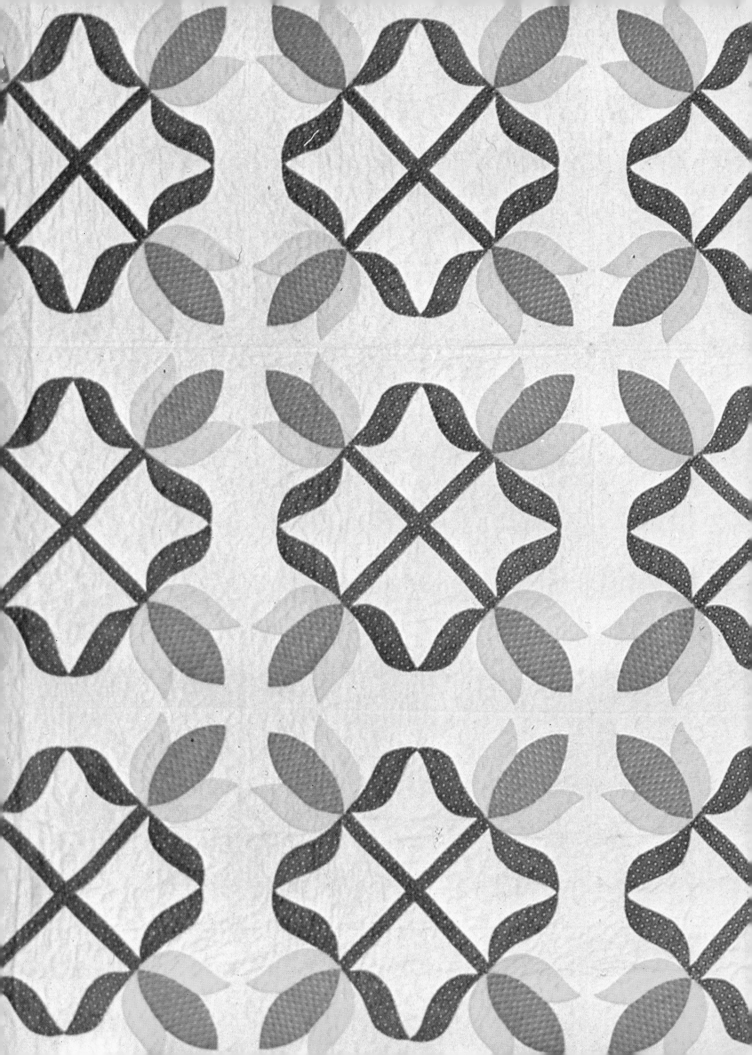